red

yellow

blue

Educators Publishing Service • DO NOT DUPLICATE

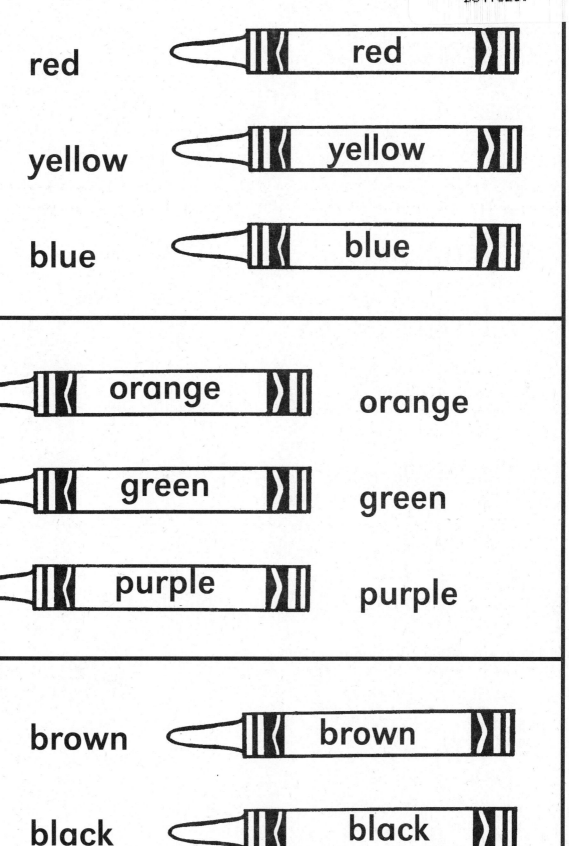

red

yellow

blue

orange

green

purple

brown

black

1

face

ace

braces

race

lace

iceberg

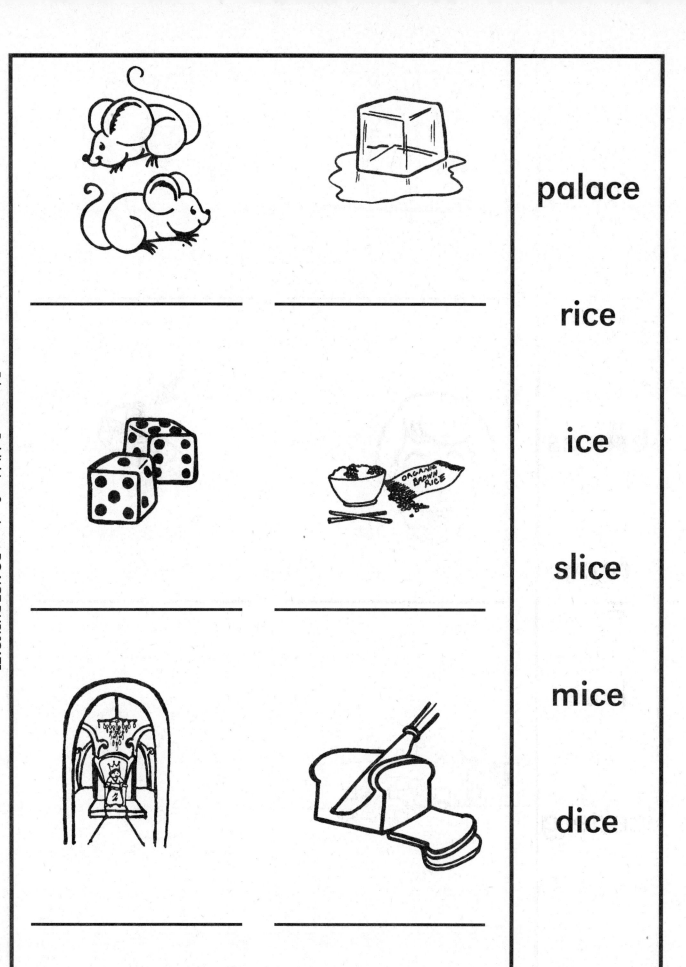

palace

rice

ice

slice

mice

dice

fence

princess

space

dancer

bracelet

prince

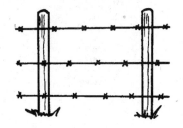

cell

celery

cent

cellar

lettuce

_____

_____

_____

The palace is black.

The dancer is purple.

The ace is yellow.

The princess is red.

The mice are brown.

The prince is blue.

_____

_____

_____

cellar   is

dancer   the

The   in

mice   See

the   dice

on   the

circle

circus

city

cider

pencil

center

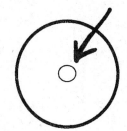

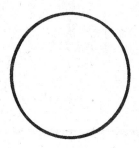

December	ice cream
fireplace	icicles
police	accident

_____   _____   _____

_____   _____   _____

9

ice

ace

_____

cider

center

_____

race

rice

_____

pencil

prince

_____

prince

princess

_____

celery

cellar

_____

circle

circus

_____

bracelet

braces

_____

unicycle   motorcycle

tricycle   bicycle

_____   _____

_____   _____

The center is brown.

The circle is orange.

The bicycle is red.

The cider is yellow.

The motorcycle is blue.

The pencil is green.

Educators Publishing Service • DO NOT DUPLICATE

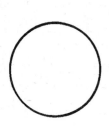

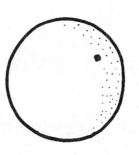

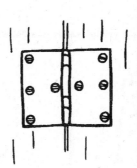

orange

hinge

cage

gem

page

angel

stage

13

baggage   orange

cabbage   lounge

garbage can

_____   _____

_____   _____

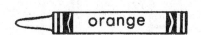

_____   _____

stagecoach   garbage

bandage   garage

refrigerator

_____   _____

_____

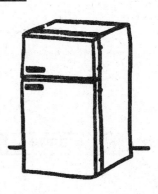

_____   _____

The lounge is blue.

The angel is orange.

The cage is red.

The stagecoach is brown.

The refrigerator is green.

The gem is yellow.

the   gem

is   The

stage   on

cabbage   The

on   is

the   cage

garbage

garage

_____

bracelet

bicycle

_____

bandage

baggage

_____

stage

space

_____

cabbage

cage

_____

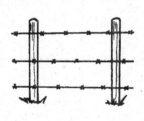

fence

face

_____

pencil

page

_____

luggage

lounge

_____

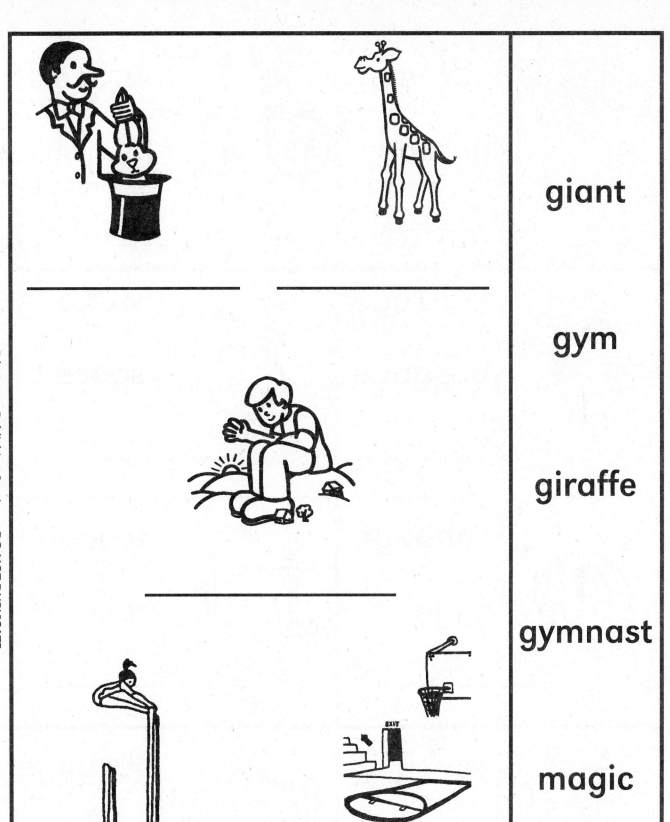

giant

gym

giraffe

gymnast

magic

The fireplace is yellow.

The bandage is orange.

The gym is brown.

The stage is green.

The ice skate is blue.

The garage is red.

judge

hedge

badge

pledge

edge

fudge

bridge

_____

_____

_____

The fudge is brown.

The badge is yellow.

The giraffe is brown.

The bridge is blue.

The gymnast is red.

The giant is green.

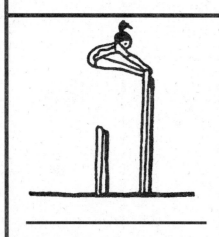
_____

_____

_____

coach

stage

skate

ice

yield

tier

field

piece

pierce

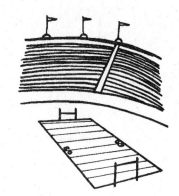

diesel

pier

thief

shield

chief

cookie   collie

candies   brownie

daisies

 _____

 _____

 _____

 _____

_____

| berries | puppies |
| pennies | bunnies |

fifties

_____

_____

_____

_____

_____

diesel

pierce

_____

bunnies

berries

_____

tier

thief

_____

fifties

field

_____

collie

cookie

_____

pier

piece

_____

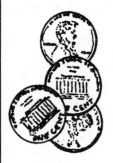

pennies

puppies

_____

candies

chief

_____

_____

_____

_____

The cookie is red.

The thief is green.

The field is blue.

The tier is brown.

The brownie is purple.

The shield is yellow.

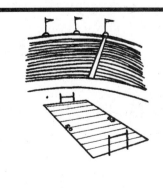
_____

_____

_____

Educators Publishing Service • DO NOT DUPLICATE

	Yes	No
Is the brownie on the bicycle?		
Is the chief in the hedge?		
Is the collie in the hedge?		
Is the collie on the bicycle?		
Is the chief on the pier?		
Is the brownie on the pier?		

The brownie is blue.

The bicycle is black.

The chief is green.

The collie is brown.

The hedge is yellow.

The pier is red.

thief   The

in   the

cell   is

The   in

stagecoach   is

brownie   the

cowboy

boy

toys

boys

cowboy
hat

cowboy
boot

Educators Publishing Service • DO NOT DUPLICATE

noise

poison

coins

point

embroider

oil well

boil

The poison is red.

The boot is black.

The toys are blue.

The boy is green.

The coins are yellow.

The cowboy is brown.

cow

girl

boy

cow

35

boil

boy

boys

well

oil

point

poison

boot   is

The   cowgirl

in   the

Educators Publishing Service • DO NOT DUPLICATE

hat   in

the   The

toys   are

_____

_____

_____

The puppies are red.

The mice are brown.

The daisies are yellow.

The bunnies are black.

The pennies are orange.

The oil well is green.

Educators Publishing Service • DO NOT DUPLICATE

_____

_____

_____

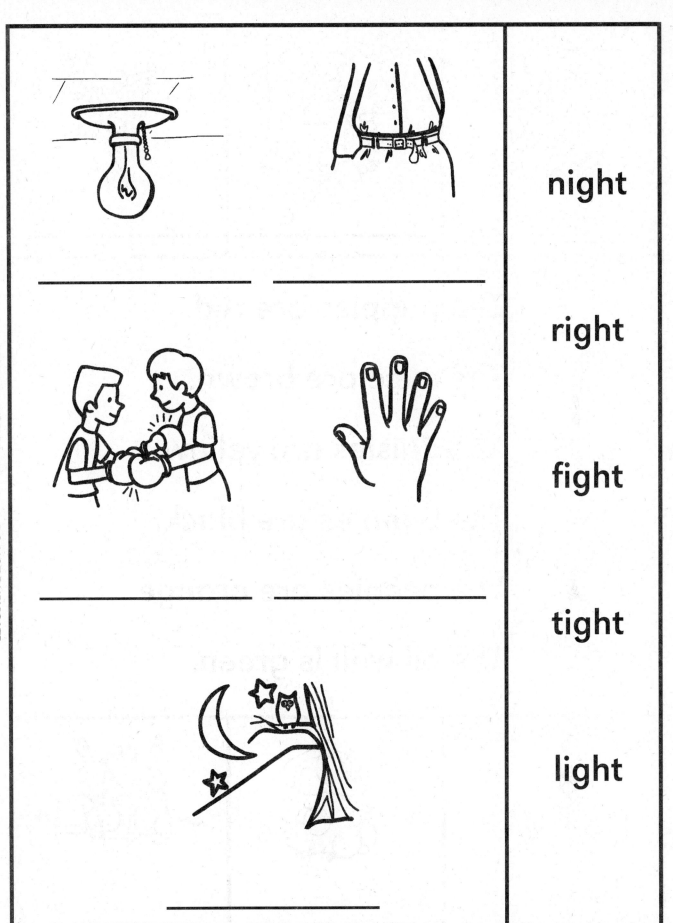

night

right

fight

tight

light

taillight   lightning

midnight   stoplight

flashlight

_____

_____

_____

_____

_____

nightmare   right

lighthouse   frighten

nightgown

_____

_____

_____

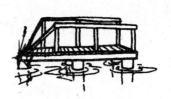

The ice skate is blue.

The pier is brown.

The ace is yellow.

The taillight is red.

The stoplight is black.

The rice is green.

Educators Publishing Service • DO NOT DUPLICATE

flashlight

frighten

lighthouse

lightning

nightgown

nightmare

right

light

photograph   microphone

telephone   pharmacist

dolphin

_____

_____

_____

gopher   elephant

trophy   alphabet

siphon

_____

_____

_____

pharmacy   earphone

megaphone   phonograph

_____

_____

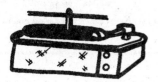

_____

_____

gopher   in

is   the

The   trophy

cow   is

The   cowboy

on   the

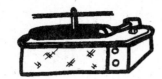

_____   _____   _____

The trophy is purple.

The elephant is yellow.

The gopher is brown.

The phonograph is red.

The dolphin is blue.

The telephone is green.

_____   _____   _____

faucet

astronaut

saucer

vault

soy sauce

_____

_____

_____

_____

_____

August   autograph

sausage   autumn

automobile

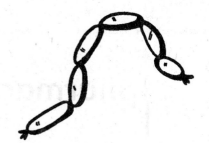

saucer

sausage

photograph

phonograph

alphabet

astronaut

pharmacist

pharmacy

The flashlight is yellow.

The nightgown is blue.

The microphone is red.

The faucet is green.

The lighthouse is brown.

The dolphin is black.

	Yes	No
Is the astronaut on the saucer?		
Is the celery on the elephant?		
Is the astronaut on the moon?		
Is the boy on the moon?		
Is the celery on the saucer?		
Is the boy on the elephant?		

The elephant is black.

The saucer is red.

The moon is yellow.

The celery is brown.

The astronaut is blue.

The boy is green.

newsstand

_____ _____

stew

newscaster

_____ _____

jewelry

newspaper

_____

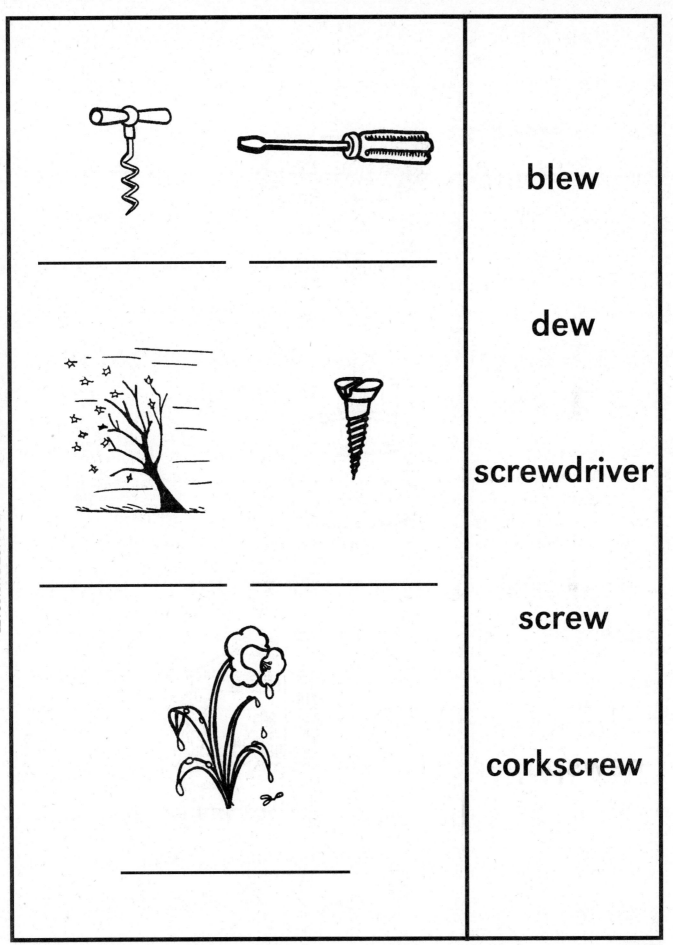

blew

dew

screwdriver

screw

corkscrew

saucer

sausage

_____

microphone

moon

_____

automobile

autumn

_____

giant

gopher

_____

pharmacy

photograph

_____

blew

siphon

_____

elephant

earphone

newsstand

nightgown

_____

shirt

night

screw

driver

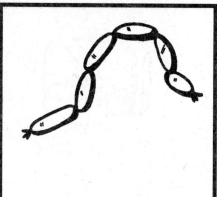

_____

_____

_____

The earphone is green.

The screwdriver is blue.

The astronaut is yellow.

The jewelry is orange.

The sausage is brown.

The newspaper is red.

Educators Publishing Service • DO NOT DUPLICATE

_____

_____

_____

		bandage
		baggage
		autograph
		autumn
		garbage
		garage
		lounge
		lettuce

cow   gopher   mice

elephant   dolphin   giraffe

_____ _____ _____

_____ _____ _____

	Yes	No
Is the giraffe in the garage?		
Is the orange in the rice?		
Is the prince on the newspaper?		
Is the prince in the garage?		
Is the orange on the newspaper?		
Is the giraffe in the rice?		

The rice is blue.

The garage is brown.

The orange is orange.

The newspaper is red.

The prince is green.

The giraffe is black.

teacher   prince   fireplace

police officer   astronaut   princess

_____   _____   _____

_____   _____   _____

rice   fudge

celery   lettuce

orange

_____   _____

_____

_____   _____

soil		
boil	_____	_____

poison		
point	_____	_____

toys		
boys	_____	_____

well		
oil	_____	_____

screwdriver in
the   is
vault   The

The   on
the   dolphin
is   newspaper

_____

_____

_____

The vault is red.

The dew is brown.

The jewelry is blue.

The newsstand is green.

The new toys are yellow.

The newscaster is orange.

Educators Publishing Service • DO NOT DUPLICATE

_____

_____

_____

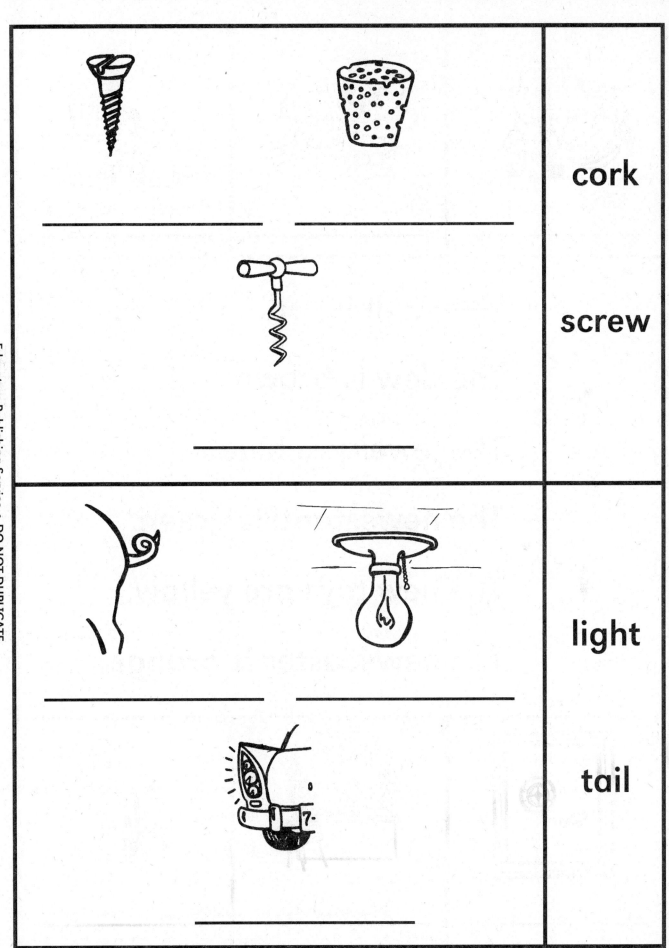

cork

screw

_____

light

tail

_____

old

sold

gold

cold

fold

goldfish

_____

told

fold

_____

hold

bold

_____

_____ _____ _____

The princess is blue.

The gold is green.

The goldfish is black.

The automobile is red.

The soy sauce is brown.

The megaphone is yellow.

_____ _____ _____

bill

fold

fish

gold

pharmacy

jewelry

drugstore

_____

_____

binoculars

pierce

stab

_____

_____

scare

saucer

frighten

_____

_____

outerspace

space

tier

_____

_____

phone

thief

telephone

_____

_____

basement

gopher

cellar

_____

_____

baggage

pennies

luggage

_____

_____

bicycle

shirt

bike

_____

_____

Educators Publishing Service • DO NOT DUPLICATE

traffic light
stoplight
gold

_____

_____

evening
cider
night

_____

_____

photograph
orange
picture

_____

_____

accident
crash
lounge

_____

_____

$3 \times 2 = 6$

$2\overline{)\dfrac{4}{8}}$ $\dfrac{4}{-\ 1}{3}$

mathematics
arithmetic
brown

_____

_____

autumn
collie
fall

_____

_____

grocery store
supermarket
fight

_____

_____

braces
dirt
soil

_____

_____

goldfish   in
is   the
megaphone The

bunnies on
are   gold
The   the

Yes No

Are the puppies in the nightshirt? _____

Is the gopher in the hat? _____

Are the puppies in the hat? _____

Is the cow in the soy sauce? _____

Is the gopher in the soy sauce? _____

Is the cow in the nightshirt? _____

The soy sauce is yellow.

The nightshirt is blue.

The hat is green.

The cow is black.

The puppies are red.

The gopher is brown.

fence phone	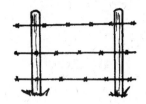	
fifties pharmacy	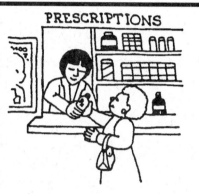	
flashlight phonograph		
photograph frighten		

taillight   automobile

driver   siphon

accident

_____   _____

_____   _____

_____

boy girl		
daylight night		
awake asleep		
hot cold		

78

Educators Publishing Service • DO NOT DUPLICATE

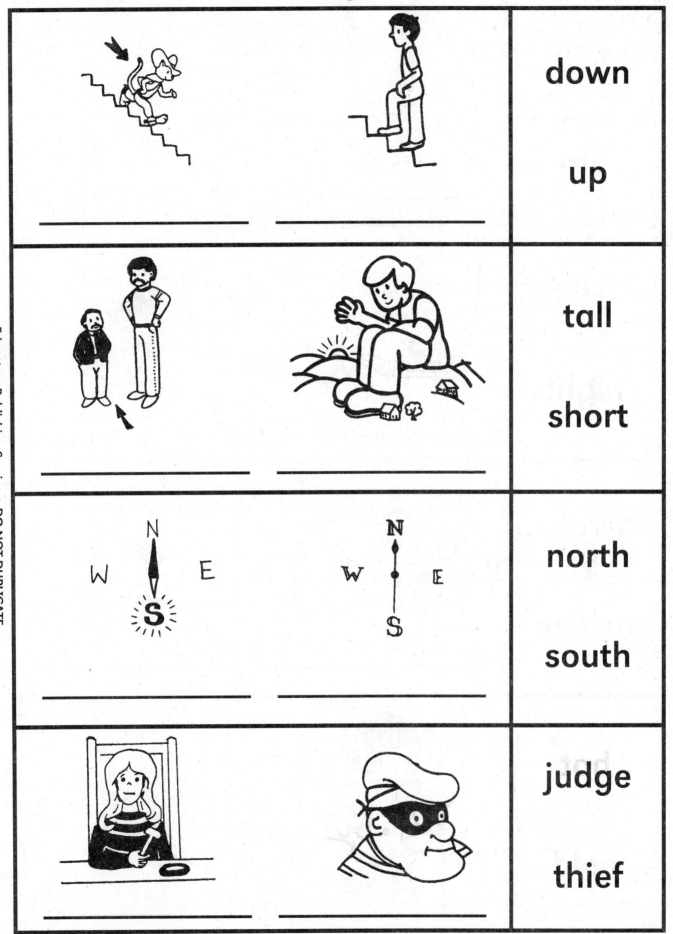

down

up

tall

short

north

south

judge

thief

_____ _____ _____

The oil well is red.

The fifties are green.

The elephant is blue.

The lightning is yellow.

The berries are black.

The candies are purple.

_____ _____ _____